The
OUT COME
of
Divine Wisdom

"Wisdom is the principal thing; therefore get wisdom: and with all thy getting get understanding."

Proverb 4:7

by

Franklin N. Abazie

The Outcome of Divine Wisdom
COPYRIGHT 2019 *by* Franklin N Abazie
ISBN: 978-0-9966-263-9-2

All right reserved. This book or any portion thereof may not be reproduced or used in any manner whatsoever without the express written permission of the publisher, except for the use of brief quotations in a book review. All Bible quotes are from King James Version and others as noted.

Published by:
F N ABAZIE PUBLISHING HOUSE---a.k.a,
Empowerment Bookstore:

That I may publish with the voice of thanksgiving and tell of all thy wondrous works.
Psalms 26:7

To order additional copies, wholesales or booking:
Call the Church office (973-372-7518)
or Empowerment Bookstore Hotline 973-393-8518

Worship address:
343 Sanford Avenue Newark New Jersey 07106
Administrative Head Office address:
33 Schley Street Newark New Jersey 07112
Email: pastorfranknto@yahoo.com
Website www.fnabaziehealingministries.org
Publishing House: www.fnabaziepublishinghouse.org

This book is a production of F N Abazie Publishing House. A publication Arms of Miracle of God Ministries 2019
Revised Edition

CONTENTS

The Mandate of The Commission......................iv

Arms of The Commission v

Favor Confession vi

Introduction..viii

CHAPTER 1
What is Wisdom? 51

CHAPTER 2
Sources of Divine Wisdom 63

CHAPTER 3
Prayer of Salvation.. 103

CHAPTER 4
About The Author 112

Books By Rev Franklin N Abazie.................. 115

The Outcome of Divine Wisdom

THE MANDATE OF THE COMMISSION

"THE MOMENT IS DUE TO IMPACT YOUR WORLD THROUGH THE REVIVAL OF THE HEALING & MIRACLE MINISTRY OF JESUS CHRIST OF NAZARETH."

"I AM SENDING YOU TO RESTORE HEALTH UNTO THEE AND I WILL HEAL THEE OF THY WOUNDS, SAID THE LORD OF HOST."

ARMS OF THE COMMISSION

1) F N Abazie Ministries-Miracle of God Ministries (Miracle Chapel Intl)
2) F N Abazie TV Ministries: Global Television Ministry Outreach.
3) F N Abazie Radio Ministries: Radio Broadcasting Outreach.
4) F N Abazie Publishing House: Book Publication.
5) F N Abazie Bible School: also called Word of Healing Bible School (W.O.H.B.S)
6) F N Abazie Evangelistic Ass: Miracle of God Ministries: Global Crusade
7) Empowerment Bookstore: Book distribution.
8) F N Abazie Helping Hands: Meeting the help of the needy world wide
9) F N Abazie Disaster Recovery Mission: Global Disaster Recovery.
10) F N Abazie Prison Ministry: Prison Ministry for all convicts "Second chance"

Some of our ministry arms are waiting the appointed time to commence.

The Outcome of Divine Wisdom

FAVOR CONFESSION

Father thank you for making me righteous and accepted through the blood of Jesus Christ. Because of that, I am blessed and highly favored by God. I am the subject of your affection. Your favor surrounds me as a shield, and the first thing that people see around me is your favored shield.

Thank you that I have favor with you and man today. All day long people go out of their way to bless me and help me. I have favor with everyone that I deal with today. Doors that were once closed are now opened for me. I receive preferential treatment, and I have special privileges, I am Gods favored child.

No good thing will he withhold from me. Because of Gods favor my enemies cannot triumph over my life. I have supernatural increase and promotion. I declare restoration to everything that the devil has stolen

Favor Confession

from my life. I have honor in the midst of my adversaries and an increase in assets, especially in real estate and expansion of territories.

Because I am highly favored by God, I experience great victories, supernatural turnarounds, and miraculous breakthrough in the midst of great impossibilities. I receive recognition, prominence, and honor. Petitions are granted to me even by ungodly authorities. Policies, rules, regulations, and laws are changed and reverse on my behalf.

I win battles that I don't even have to fight, because God fights them for me. This is the day, the set time and the designated moment for me to experience the free favor of God, that profusely and lavishly abound on my behalf in Jesus name. **Amen.**

The Outcome of Divine Wisdom

INTRODUCTION

"Wisdom hath builded her house, she hath hewn out her seven pillars." **Proverb 9:1**

"Wisdom is the principal thing; therefore get wisdom: and with all thy getting get understanding." Proverb4:7

I may never get the chance to meet with you face to face. But I am glad you picked up a copy of this book. Often we blame the devil for every atrocity we see today around the world. Honestly in my opinion it is because of ignorant-By this I mean lack of divine wisdom. The entire world lack *the wisdom of God.* So many of us lack the wisdom of God.

For some time now, I have been applying divine wisdom into my life step by step. A little here a little there. I would like to share most of my convictions in the

word of God with you today. *Wisdom is the principal thing; therefore get wisdom: and with all thy getting get understanding."*
If you do not have the principle thing you shall suffer punishment. Therefore it is my privilege to bring some insight on the on the wisdom of the Most High God.

There are some great benefits in divine wisdom!

Hear this....

Whatever you read is called information.

It can come by listening to an audio tape DVD, CD or watching a video or through YouTube.

Whatever you understand is called revelation

Again revelation can come through an audio tape, DVD, CD, YouTube video, or television.

But what you apply into your life is called Wisdom.

"Therefore whosoever heareth these sayings of mine, and doeth them, I will liken him unto a wise man, which built his house upon a rock." **Mathew 7:24**

"And the rain descended, and the floods came, and the winds blew, and beat upon that house; and it fell not: for it was founded upon a rock." **Mathew 7:25**

"And every one that heareth these sayings of mine, and doeth them not, shall be likened unto a foolish man, which built his house upon the sand:" **Mathew 7:26**

"And the rain descended, and the floods came, and the winds blew, and beat upon that house; and it fell: and great was the fall of it." **Mathew7:27**

Come with me let's hear what the Holy Spirit is saying to us all about restoration.

Happy Reading

HIS DESTINY WAS THE CROSS....

HIS PURPOSE WAS LOVE....

HIS REASON WAS YOU....

"For a just man falleth seven times, and riseth up again: but the wicked shall fall into mischief."

Proverb24:16

"And said to his servant, Go up now, look toward the sea. And he went up, and looked, and said, There is nothing. And he said, Go again seven times."

1king18:43

"And it came to pass at the seventh time, that he said, Behold, there ariseth a little cloud out of the sea, like a man's hand. And he said, Go up, say unto Ahab, Prepare thy chariot, and get thee down that the rain stop thee not."

1king18:44

"Then He got up and left the synagogue, and entered Simon's home Now Simon's mother-in-law was suffering from a high fever, and they asked Him to help her. And standing over her, He rebuked the fever, and it left her; and she immediately got up and waited on them."

Luke 4:38-39

"And a woman who had a hemorrhage for twelve years, and could not be healed by anyone, came up behind Him and touched the fringe of His cloak, and immediately her hemorrhage stopped."

Luke 8:43-44

"And there in front of Him was a man suffering from dropsy. And Jesus answered and spoke to the lawyers and Pharisees, saying, "Is it lawful to heal on the Sabbath, or not?" But they kept silent. And He took hold of him and healed him, and sent him away."

Luke 14:2-4

"Soon afterwards He went to a city called Nain; and His disciples were going along with Him, accompanied by a large crowd. Now as He approached the gate of the city, a dead man was being carried out, the only son of his mother, and she was a widow; and a sizeable crowd from the city was with her. When the Lord saw her, He felt compassion for her, and said to her, "Do not weep."

Luke7:11-15

"Yet even now," declares the LORD, "Return to Me with all your heart, And with fasting, weeping and mourning;"

Joel 2:12-13

"whom heaven must receive until the period of restoration of all things about which God spoke by the mouth of His holy prophets from ancient time."

Acts3:21

"Now a certain man was sick, Lazarus of Bethany, the village of Mary and her sister Martha. It was the Mary who anointed the Lord with ointment, and wiped His feet with her hair, whose brother Lazarus was sick. So the sisters sent word to Him, saying, "Lord, behold, he whom You love is sick."

John 11:1-44

"And they came to Bethsaida And they brought a blind man to Jesus and implored Him to touch him. Taking the blind man by the hand, He brought him out of the village; and after spitting on his eyes and laying His hands on him, He asked him, "Do you see anything?" And he looked up and said, "I see men, for I see them like trees, walking around."

Mark8:22-25

"As He passed by, He saw a man blind from birth. And His disciples asked Him, "Rabbi, who sinned, this man or his parents, that he would be born blind?" Jesus answered, "It was neither that this man sinned, nor his parents; but it was so that the works of God might be displayed in him."

John9:1-7

"They brought to Him one who was deaf and spoke with difficulty, and they implored Him to lay His hand on him. Jesus took him aside from the crowd, by himself, and put His fingers into his ears, and after spitting, He touched his tongue with the saliva; and looking up to heaven with a deep sigh, He said to him, "Ephphatha!" that is, "Be opened."

Mark 7:32-35

"And the wolf will dwell with the lamb, And the leopard will lie down with the young goat, And the calf and the young lion and the fatling together; And a little boy will lead them. Also the cow and the bear will graze, Their young will lie down together, And the lion will eat straw like the ox. The nursing child will play by the hole of the cobra, And the weaned child will put his hand on the viper's den."

Isaiah 11:6-9

"The afflicted and needy are seeking water, but there is none, And their tongue is parched with thirst; I, the LORD, will answer them Myself, As the God of Israel I will not forsake them. "I will open rivers on the bare heights And springs in the midst of the valleys; I will make the wilderness a pool of water And the dry land fountains of water. "I will put the cedar in the wilderness, The acacia and the myrtle and the olive tree; I will place the juniper in the desert Together with the box tree and the cypress."

Isaiah 41:17-20

"For as the rain and the snow come down from heaven, And do not return there without watering the earth And making it bear and sprout, And furnishing seed to the sower and bread to the eater; So will My word be which goes forth from My mouth; It will not return to Me empty, Without accomplishing what I desire, And without succeeding in the matter for which I sent it. "For you will go out with joy And be led forth with peace; The mountains and the hills will break forth into shouts of joy before you, And all the trees of the field will clap their hands."

Isaiah55:10-11

"Then I saw a new heaven and a new earth; for the first heaven and the first earth passed away, and there is no longer any sea. And I saw the holy city, new Jerusalem, coming down out of heaven from God, made ready as a bride adorned for her husband. And I heard a loud voice from the throne, saying, "Behold, the tabernacle of God is among men, and He will dwell among them, and they shall be His people, and God Himself will be among them."

Rev21:1-4

"Then he showed me a river of the water of life, clear as crystal, coming from the throne of God and of the Lamb, in the middle of its street On either side of the river was the tree of life, bearing twelve kinds of fruit, yielding its fruit every month; and the leaves of the tree were for the healing of the nations. There will no longer be any curse; and the throne of God and of the Lamb will be in it, and His bond-servants will serve Him."

Rev22:1-5

xxx

> *"Oh, that the salvation of Israel would come out of Zion! When the LORD restores His captive people, Jacob will rejoice, Israel will be glad."*
>
> **Psalm 14:7**

"For God will save Zion and build the cities of Judah, That they may dwell there and possess it. The descendants of His servants will inherit it, And those who love His name will dwell in it."

Psalm 69:35-36

"For I am the LORD your God, who upholds your right hand, Who says to you, 'Do not fear, I will help you."

Isaiah 41:13

"Listen to me, you who pursue righteousness, Who seek the LORD: Look to the rock from which you were hewn And to the quarry from which you were dug. "Look to Abraham your father And to Sarah who gave birth to you in pain; When he was but one I called him, Then I blessed him and multiplied him." Indeed, the LORD will comfort Zion; He will comfort all her waste places And her wilderness He will make like Eden, And her desert like the garden of the LORD; Joy and gladness will be found in her, Thanksgiving and sound of a melody."

Isaiah51:1-6

"Thus says the LORD, 'Behold, I will restore the fortunes of the tents of Jacob And have compassion on his dwelling places; And the city will be rebuilt on its ruin, And the palace will stand on its rightful place. 'From them will proceed thanksgiving And the voice of those who celebrate; And I will multiply them and they will not be diminished; I will also honor them and they will not be insignificant. 'Their children also will be as formerly, And their congregation shall be established before Me; And I will punish all their oppressors."

Jeremiah 30:18-22

"But you, O mountains of Israel, you will put forth your branches and bear your fruit for My people Israel; for they will soon come. 'For, behold, I am for you, and I will turn to you, and you will be cultivated and sown. 'I will multiply men on you, all the house of Israel, all of it; and the cities will be inhabited and the waste places will be rebuilt."

Ezekiel 36:8-12

"Behold, days are coming,"　declares the LORD, "When the plowman will overtake the reaper And the treader of grapes him who sows seed; When the mountains will drip sweet wine And all the hills will be dissolved. "Also I will restore the captivity of My people Israel, And they will rebuild the ruined cities and live in them; They will also plant vineyards and drink their wine, And make gardens and eat their fruit. "I will also plant them on their land, And they will not again be rooted out from their land Which I have given them," Says the LORD your God."

Amos9:13-15

"For I do not want you, brethren, to be uninformed of this mystery--so that you will not be wise in your own estimation--that a partial hardening has happened to Israel until the fullness of the Gentiles has come in; and so all Israel will be saved; just as it is written, "THE DELIVERER WILL COME FROM ZION, HE WILL REMOVE UNGODLINESS FROM JACOB." "THIS IS MY COVENANT WITH THEM, WHEN I TAKE AWAY THEIR SINS."

Romans 11:25-27

"Within three more days Pharaoh will lift up your head and restore you to your office; and you will put Pharaoh's cup into his hand according to your former custom when you were his cupbearer."

Genesis 40:13

"If you are pure and upright, Surely now He would rouse Himself for you And restore your righteous estate."

Job 8:6

"Nevertheless, I will restore their captivity, the captivity of Sodom and her daughters, the captivity of Samaria and her daughters, and along with them your own captivity."

Ezekiel 16:53

"Now it came about after this that Joash decided to restore the house of the LORD."
2Chronicle24:4

"Then we asked those elders and said to them thus, 'Who issued you a decree to rebuild this temple and to finish this structure?"

Ezra5:9

"Then David defeated Hadadezer, the son of Rehob king of Zobah, as he went to restore his rule at the River."

2samuel8:3

"But afterward I will restore The fortunes of the sons of Ammon," Declares the LORD."

Jeremiah49:6

"Return, O faithless sons, I will heal your faithlessness." "Behold, we come to You; For You are the LORD our God."
Jeremiah3:22

"I will heal their apostasy, I will love them freely, For My anger has turned away from them."

Hosea 14:4

"He will again have compassion on us; He will tread our iniquities under foot Yes, You will cast all their sins Into the depths of the sea."

Micah 7:19

"I have seen his ways, but I will heal him; I will lead him and restore comfort to him and to his mourners."

Isaiah57:18

*"For I will restore you to health
And I will heal you of your
wounds,' declares the LORD,
'Because they have called
you an outcast, saying: "It is
Zion; no one cares for her."*

Jeremiah30:17

CHAPTER 1

WHAT IS WISDOM?

"Wisdom is the principal thing; therefore get wisdom: and with all thy getting get understanding."

Proverb4:7

Divine *wisdom* is the application of *the word of God*. If iam permitted to put it this way;The commandment of God that we obey, will make us a commander inlife

"Wisdom hath built her house, she hath hewn out her seven pillars." **Proverb 9:1**

"I wisdom dwell with prudence, and find out knowledge of witty inventions." **Proverb 8:12**

The Outcome of Divine Wisdom

Whatever you hear, read or watch is called information.

These days you can get all kinds of information at the click of a button *on your phone or home computer. Contrary to what you may be thinking,* **whatever you understand thoroughly is called revelation.** God said to Abraham the other day that as far as your eyes can see." *For all the land which thou seest, to thee will I give it, and to thy seed forever."*

Whatever you heard, understand and apply into your life is what I call wisdom.

If I am permitted to put it this way… *you only understand what you heard by applying it into your life. That is Divine Wisdom.*

We hear a lot of things daily. We listen and see or watch a lot of things daily. *But how many of those relevant information do we apply into our lives?*

CHAPTER 1 : What is Wisdom?

Simply put… Divine wisdom is the application of relevant information into our life. In a known definition of one of my great mentors in the faith… He said ***Wisdom is your ability to recognize difference.***

Difference in people, difference in times, difference in season, and difference in your gift or talent. Etc.

Wisdom is the principal thing; therefore get wisdom: and with all thy getting get understanding. **Proverb 4:7**

Wisdom strengtheneth the wise more than ten mighty men which are in the city. **Eccl 7:19**

"Wisdom hath built her house, she hath hewn out her seven pillars." **Proverb 9:1**

"I wisdom dwell with prudence, and find out knowledge of witty inventions." **Proverb 8:12**

The Outcome of Divine Wisdom

God designed the entire world to operate by wisdom. If you are in trouble, it is because you lack wisdom.

Hear this…..

"A prudent man foreseeth the evil, and hideth himself; but the simple pass on, and are punished." **Proverb27:12**

A prudent man foreseeth the evil, and hideth himself: but the simple pass on, and are punished. **Proverb22:3**

If you have succeeded in life, it is because you have applied Divine wisdom into your life. *"If any of you lack wisdom, let him ask of God, that giveth to all men liberally, and upbraideth not; and it shall be given him."* **James1:5**

You are not poor because God made you poor, or because there is a curse over your life. You are poor because you lack wisdom.

CHAPTER 1 : What is Wisdom?

You are poor because you make poor choices in life.

You financed a vehicle with your credit. You did not check how much it will cost you to pay off on that *vehicle*. You saw a beautiful girl and rushed into *marriage,* you did not know-her character or how she handles finance. *You did not ask God before make such life changing choices into your life*. We were told… *He that getteth wisdom loveth his own soul: he that keepeth understanding shall find good.*

"Delight is not seemly for a fool; much less for a servant to have rule over princes." Proverb19:10

"The discretion of a man deferreth his anger; and it is his glory to pass over a transgression." Proverb19:11

"A foolish son is the calamity of his father: and the contentions of a wife are a continual dropping." Proverb19:13

The Outcome of Divine Wisdom

"House and riches are the inheritance of fathers: and a prudent wife is from the Lord." **Proverb19:14**

"Slothfulness casteth into a deep sleep; and an idle soul shall suffer hunger." **Proverb19:15**

"He that keepeth the commandment keepeth his own soul; but he that despiseth his ways shall die." **Proverb19:16**

"He that hath pity upon the poor lendeth unto the Lord; and that which he hath given will he pay him again." **Proverb19:17**

"Chasten thy son while there is hope, and let not thy soul spare for his crying." **Proverb19:18**

LET EXAMINE THESE KEY SCRIPTURES AS A CASE STUDY

------------Do not be ignorant--------------

CHAPTER 1 : What is Wisdom?

Anger has Power to keep us into bondage.

" A man of great wrath shall suffer punishment: for if thou deliver him, yet thou must do it again." Proverb19:19

Fools remain in trouble and in penury because they lack wisdom.

"Fools because of their transgression, and because of their iniquities, are afflicted." Psalm107:17

A fool can become wiseas long as they apply Gods wisdom into their life.

"Even a fool, when he holdeth his peace, is counted wise: and he that shutteth his lips is esteemed a man of understanding." **Proverb17:28**

What then is Divine Wisdom?

The American heritage college dictionary defines *wisdom as understanding*

The Outcome of Divine Wisdom

of what is true, right or lasting; insight. Common sense, good judgment. The sum of scholarly learning through the ages; knowledge. Wise teaching of the ancient sages. In my own view, I defined wisdom as knowing the scriptural ordained way of doing everything in one's life and doing them.

Jesus defined wisdom in Mathew7:24 thus whosoever heareth these saying of mine, and doeth them, I will liken him unto a wise man, which built his house upon a rock.

Divine wisdom is not common sense--it is scriptural sense. Simple *define the obedience and applications of scripture into your life equals to divine wisdom.* No one can walk in divine wisdom without material prove to show for it.

"And it shall come to pass, if thou shalt hearken diligently unto the voice of the

CHAPTER 1 : What is Wisdom?

LORD thy God, to observe and to do all his commandments which I command thee this day, that the LORD thy God will set thee on high above all nations of the earth: And all these blessings shall come on thee, and overtake thee, if thou shalt hearken unto the voice of the LORD thy God. Blessed shalt thou be in the city, and blessed shalt thou be in the field. Blessed shall be the fruit of thy body, and the fruit of thy ground, and the fruit of thy cattle, the increase of thy kine, and the flocks of thy sheep. Blessed shall be thy basket and thy store. Blessed shalt thou be when thou comest in, and blessed shalt thou be when thou goest out." **Deut28:1-5**

We all know that the fear of the Lord is the beginning of wisdom. (See Psalms111:10, Proverb 9:10, Proverb1:7).

But how many people can truly say yes! I do apply the word of God into my life on a daily basis?

The Outcome of Divine Wisdom

It is wisdom to know what the word of God is saying on any issue of life. Everyone must crave for the wisdom of God. It is good to go to school, for education which is secular or man's wisdom received as a result of learning gives you information. *It is the application of that acquired information equal divine wisdom.* In my own understanding lack of divine wisdom guarantees poverty sickness and disease.

"My people are destroyed for lack of knowledge: because thou hast rejected knowledge, I will also reject thee, that thou shalt be no priest to me: seeing thou hast forgotten the law of thy God, I will also forget thy children." **Hosea 4:6**

"Therefore my people are gone into captivity, because they have no knowledge: and their honourable men are famished, and their multitude dried up with thirst." **Isaiah 5:13**

CHAPTER 1 : What is Wisdom?

a different kinds of wisdom.

1) *Divine wisdom of God:*

Believe me, the wisdom that is from above is all we need today.

" But the wisdom that is from above is first pure, then peaceable, gentle, and easy to be intreated, full of mercy and good fruits, without partiality, and without hypocrisy." **James3:17**

2) *Devilish wisdom:*

This wisdom is the power the occultist use, it is diabolic and destructive. Reject this wisdom with all your understanding. This is the devils wisdom responsible for all the nightmares, torture, and oppression. **James3:15** This wisdom descendeth not from above, but is earthly, sensual, devilish

3) *Sensual Wisdom:*

The Outcome of Divine Wisdom

Simple defined, this is acquired information.

This is intellectual wisdom, inspired by God by innovated by man for improvement of the life and the welfare of mankind. This is the wisdom behind scientific innovation and all modern invention and technological changes.

If you learn to know what God is saying per-time in your life you will forever come out of trouble. I pray-Go for divine wisdom and change your life forever.

Divine wisdom therefore means doing the right thing at the right time. Never let the devil deceive you again. If you are in business, pick up the right book and read about business. If you are in trading-pick up a good book about trading and read it. Constantly learn to improve your life. I see God changing your level. I see you breaking through.

CHAPTER 2
SOURCES OF DIVINE WISDOM

"But the wisdom that is from above is first pure, then peaceable, gentle, and easy to be intreated, full of mercy and good fruits, without partiality, and without hypocrisy."

James 3:17

Contrary to what the secular world believe, divine wisdom is from God.

In the secular world you go to school to receive information but it is divine wisdom that gives us revelation to change our world. I call this revelation divine ideas. Divine ideas are not only creative and innovative but it exalts, and prosper in life.

The Outcome of Divine Wisdom

It does no matter what the scholars and scientist have discovered in their theories, facts, and data. The bible is the foundation for all those findings.

Paul said O Timothy, keep that which is committed to thy trust, avoiding profane and vain babblings, and oppositions of science falsely so called.

Divine wisdom is not from man or acquired from any school of thought and learning; But divine wisdom is from God. "If any of you lack wisdom, let him ask of God, that giveth to all men liberally, and upbraideth not; and it shall be given him". **James1:5**

This wisdom is hidden in the word of God. Once you have discovered it there shall be a reward. *My son, eat thou honey, because it is good; and the honeycomb, which is sweet to thy taste: So shall the knowledge of wisdom be unto thy soul: when*

CHAPTER 2 : Sources of Divine Wisdom

thou hast found it, then there shall be a reward, and thy expectation shall not be cut off. **Proverb 24:13-14**

The outstanding benefits of divine wisdom are unaccountable. In fact the whole universe is standing by reason of divine wisdom.

The bible says *"....He upholding all things by the word of his power.* **Hebrew 1:3**

The world was founded by Gods divine wisdom. (See Proverb 3:19).

And the earth was without form, and void; and darkness was upon the face of the deep. And the Spirit of God moved upon the face of the waters. And God said, Let there be light: and there was light. **Genesis 1:2-3**

This light is Gods divine creative wisdom

The Outcome of Divine Wisdom

1) *Divine wisdom is profitable*: Eccl 10:10 ....but wisdom is profitable to direct.

2) *Divine wisdom guarantees strength:* Wisdom strengtheneth the wise more than ten mighty men which are in the city. **Eccl 7:19**

3) *Divine wisdom is creative:* "The LORD by wisdom hath founded the earth; by understanding hath he established the heavens". **Proverb 3:19**

4) *Divine wisdom is in treatable*: "But the wisdom that is from above is first pure, then peaceable, gentle, and easy to be intreated."

Proverb 3:12 Happy is the man that findeth wisdom, and the man that getteth understanding.

The wisdom of God is available for everyone. The good news is it is free for

CHAPTER 2 : Sources of Divine Wisdom

everyone that believes. This wisdom brings excellence and it prospers in every endeavor of life. Your life will always remain in absolute obscurity and despair until divine ideas come alive in your mental system.

"a man's wisdom maketh his face to shine, and the boldness of his face shall be changed." **Eccl8:1**

Although the fear of the Lord is the beginning of wisdom and to depart from evil is understanding, Nevertheless, the wisdom of God is the custodian of knowledge, it is creative, it is pure and in treatable. It is the wisdom of God that makes a man destiny.

No man can make a mark on earth without the help of God. The help of God is the grace of God and the wisdom of God is the unfolding of God's grace unto anyone who desire it. "If any of you lack wisdom, let him ask of God, that giveth to all men liberally, and upbraideth not; and it shall be given him." **James1:5**

How Do I receive impartation of Divine Wisdom?

1) *By laying of hands by your mentor; prophets/pastor*:

"And Joshua the son of Nun was full of the spirit of wisdom; for Moses had laid his hands upon him: and the children of Israel hearkened unto him, and did as the LORD commanded Moses. " Deut34:9.

God's grace is imparted unto a person once hands are laid unto them. "Neglect not the gift that is in thee, which was given thee by prophecy, with the laying on of the hands of the presbytery." 1tim4:14

2) *By learning and studying:*

Studying books and materials of your mentors, and reviewing written material will

CHAPTER 2 : Sources of Divine Wisdom

impart the Spirit of wisdom; *"Till I come, give attendance to reading, to exhortation, to doctrine."* **1tim4:13** "Study to shew thyself approved unto God, a workman that needeth not to be ashamed, rightly dividing the word of truth." **2tim2:15**

3) *By training and mentorship:*

Elijah mentored Elisha and the mantle of Elijah fell on Elisha. "And Elijah took his mantle, and wrapped it together, and smote the waters, and they were divided hither and thither, so that they two went over on dry ground." **2King2:8**

"And he took the mantle of Elijah that fell from him, and smote the waters, and said, Where is the LORD God of Elijah? and when he also had smitten the waters, they parted hither and thither: and Elisha went over." **2king2:14**

Pray Lord open me up with the mystery of wisdom, grant me divine wisdom like

unto Solomon to run the race of life, to answer my call with all diligence all the days of my life, in Jesus Name. Amen

It is interesting to reveal unto all believers that the power of faith is hidden in obedience. This obedience is the mystery that humbled Jesus Christ unto death, even the death of the cross. (See Philippians 2:7-8).

The punishment of Adam and Eve from the Garden of Eden did not only ended in sowing confusion and anarchy to mankind, but also brought shame, hardship, difficulties, and struggle unto man. Jesus Christ came out of His obedience to redeem and rescue from the horrors of life.

Despite challenges and obstacles facing us today, God gave us wisdom to do the right thing. *What is the right thing?* You must be born again.

CHAPTER 2 : Sources of Divine Wisdom

If any man be in Christ out of true obedience he is a new creature. (See 2cor5:17). Until you understand the mystery of obedience you remain a prey unto the devil.

What is Obedience?

Whatever God tell you to do, do it whole heartedly for it is obedience. "His mother saith unto the servants, whatsoever he saith unto you, do it. **John2:5**

Jesus said "Therefore whosoever heareth these sayings of mine, and doeth them, I will liken him unto a wise man, which built his house upon a rock. **Mathew7:24**

The *wisdom of God* is hidden in *your obedience to the word of God.* It is your obedience to the word of God that validates your faith in God. If your life has been full of sorrows and errors, set back, and difficulties, it means there is something you are not doing right. If you have done everything right and nothing is still working for you, then you must go to God on the altar of prayers

Impartation of Divine Wisdom through the power of Obedience

"If they obey and serve him, they shall spend their days in prosperity, and their years in pleasures." **Job36:11**

Obedience is a secret, hidden in the mysteries of the kingdom of God. God has made it clear in scriptures that if you obey, He shall bless!!Everyone desire to be great, but nobody want to obey the principles, no one want to follow the law nor obey the statue of the Lord. Although Obedience is a kingdom mystery of changing levels; nevertheless, obedience will not produce without faith. For without faith it is impossible to please God.

CHAPTER 2 : Sources of Divine Wisdom

Abraham obeyed God and was mightily blessed.

"Now the LORD had said unto Abram, Get thee out of thy country, and from thy kindred, and from thy father's house, unto a land that I will show thee: And I will make of thee a great nation, and I will bless thee, and make thy name great; and thou shalt be a blessing: And I will bless them that bless thee, and curse him that curseth thee: and in thee shall all families of the earth be blessed. So Abram departed, as the LORD had spoken unto him; and Lot went with him: and Abram was seventy and five years old when he departed out of Haran. "**Genesis 12:1-4**

Peter Obeyed Jesus and caught a boat sinking, record breaking-fish

"And saw two ships standing by the lake: but the fishermen were gone out of them, and were washing their nets. And he entered into one of the ships, which was Simon's, and prayed him that he would thrust out a little from the land. And he sat down, and taught the people out of the ship. Now when he had left speaking, he said unto Simon, Launch out into the deep, and let down your nets for a draught. And Simon answering said unto him, Master, we have toiled all the night, and have taken nothing: nevertheless at thy word I will let down the net. And when they had this done, they inclosed a great multitude of fishes: and their net brake. And they beckoned unto their partners, which were in the other ship, that they should come and help them. And they came, and filled both the ships, so that they began to sink." **Luke5:2-7**

Jonah disobeyed God and was swallowed by the fish for three days and three nights.

CHAPTER 2 : Sources of Divine Wisdom

The question here today is Are Have you been living in obedience to the word of God? **Or you have been living in disobedience of the laws and statue of God.**

It is clearly written in Isaiah1:19-20

"If ye be willing and obedient, ye shall eat the good of the land; But if ye refuse and rebel, ye shall be devoured with the sword: for the mouth of the LORD hath spoken it." Isaiah1:19

God has spoken in time past, God has made it clear in His word and even today through His Holy Prophets in time of old and even now through this book. Your life will worth nothing until you return to obey God.

All your personal efforts will amount to nothing if you will not receive a new heart to obey God today. *Think of it? What will it profit you if you gain the whole world and loses your soul?*

The Outcome of Divine Wisdom

Perhaps God has called you into the evangelical ministry or into the gospel music ministry, or may be into the preaching and healing ministry; *the big question here is do you have faith to and the obedience to answer the call of God in your life today?*

Obey God today and he will bless your life forever. He will bless your water and your bread. (See exodus23:25-26).

Do you want to see trouble before you obey God?

"And it came to pass, when Pharaoh had let the people go, that God led them not through the way of the land of the Philistines, although that was near; for God said, Lest peradventure the people repent when they see war, and they return to Egypt." **Exodus3:17**

CHAPTER 2 : Sources of Divine Wisdom

The rich fool lived in disobedience.

"And he said, This will I do: I will pull down my barns, and build greater; and there will I bestow all my fruits and my goods. And I will say to my soul, Soul, thou hast much goods laid up for many years; take thine ease, eat, drink, and be merry. But God said unto him, Thou fool, this night thy soul shall be required of thee: then whose shall those things be, which thou hast provided?" **Luke12:18-20**

Obey God and return unto him. Obey the word of God today and watch God turn your whole life around. Amen!

Wisdom demand obedience to the word of God.

It is important to understand that the secret of obedience is hidden in faith. *"For as the body without the spirit is dead, so faith without works is dead also."* **James2:26**

The bible teaches that whatsoever is not faith is sin. Our heart is the engine room of our life. It is important to note that *out of the heart flows the issues of life.* David said Thy word have I hid in mine heart, that I might not sin against thee.

The easiest place for the enemy to attack you- *is your heart*.

Paul said: *For with the heart man believeth unto righteousness.* Until all your thought are brought into captivity to the obedience of Christ you will remain a prey and a victim in the hand of the enemy.

What do I mean by Obedience?

So many of us have disobeyed God out of ignorance. Without understanding we are bound to disobey God. *God is spirit and must be worshiped in spirit and in truth.*

CHAPTER 2 : Sources of Divine Wisdom

The first outcome of obedience is your salvation.

Are you truly saved?

For if any man be in Christ He is a new creature. (See2cor5:17).Until you become a child of God, you will struggle with frustration, depression, anger lack and want.

How do I become a child of God?

"Jesus answered and said unto him, Verily, verily, I say unto thee, Except a man be born again, he cannot see the kingdom of God. Nicodemus saith unto him, How can a man be born when he is old? can he enter the second time into his mother's womb, and be born? **John3:3-4**

"Jesus answered, Verily, verily, I say unto thee, Except a man be born of water and of the Spirit, he cannot enter into the kingdom of God. That which is born of the flesh is flesh; and that which is born of the Spirit is spirit." **John3:5**

"The Spirit itself beareth witness with our spirit, that we are the children of God." **Romans 8:16**

The second Outcome of Obedience is the blessing of the Lord

A lot of people live in material riches yet their soul perish in anguish, in-depression, and in-sorrow and under the oppression of the wicked.

It is the blessing of the Lord that delivers the joy of the Lord. Recall the *Joy of the Lord is your strength.* (See Nehemiah8:10)

It is easy to go to the psychiatrist for prescription to make you happy. *Well they do not belong to the kingdom of God, hence, they miss it. It is blessing of the LORD, it*

CHAPTER 2 : Sources of Divine Wisdom

maketh rich, and he addeth no sorrow with it.

Well, it is medically proven that;

"A merry heart doeth good like a medicine: but a broken spirit drieth the bones." **Proverb17:22**

"But the people that do know their God shall be strong, and do exploits." **Daniel11:32**

If you know your God, then forget about cancer and blood cloth disease.

*If God be for you .***Think of It!**

Who shall be against you? Forget about it! No weapon fashioned against you shall prosper. Declare this in faith with me in the Name of Jesus. Amen

The third Outcome of Obedience is Long-life

"With long life will I satisfy him, and shew him my salvation. "Psalm91:16

"There shall nothing cast their young, nor be barren, in thy land: the number of thy days I will fulfil." **Exodus23:26**

The above scriptures above validates the provision of long life. *Jesus already took your diseases away*. All the ordinances that was against you has been nailed on the cross. Halleluiah! No barrenness is permitted in the kingdom of God.

You are destined to be fruitful, you must subdue, reproduce, and multiply. Whatever you do for a living it is destined to prosper. (See Psalm1:3) *Long life is guaranteed if you obey and serve God.*

In my definition, *obedience as the application of the wisdom of God.* I can safely conclude that *obedience* equals *divine wisdom.* (Mathew7:24-27).

CHAPTER 2 : Sources of Divine Wisdom

We understand from scriptures that is divine wisdom that distinguishes common men from great men. "Whatsoever is from above is above all" (John3:31) (also see James 3:17). Secondly, *Obedience equals signs and wonders.* "Whatsoever he saith unto you, do it". (John2:5).

Finally I *confirm that obedience equals prosperity.* (See Joshua1:8). Your current struggle is a result of your disobedience.

You may not like this but poverty, and lack has absolute power to prevail in your life *until you yield to obedience.*

It is the commandment you obey that will put you in command. *If you obey the commandment of God it will make you a commander in life.*

Until you obey the commandment of God, it is not your turn to be a financial commander. (Deuteronomy28:1-13). One bible translation says Obadiah 1:17……*and the house of Jacob shall be in command.*

Permit me therefore to make these conclusion; whereas the word of God is the author of faith, I summarize that obedience is the finisher of our faith.

Permit me to explain when I said that the word of God is the author of faith.

The bible says by the spoken words where the heaven created. (Psalm 33:6) But *Jesus is the word of God.* The word of God has given us *the authority and power to see the works of faith.* (When Jesus died on the cross and said it is finish); (John30:19, hebrews12:1-2).

It takes obedience to the word of God, to have the character and the mindset of Christ (Phillippians2:5-10).

CHAPTER 2 : Sources of Divine Wisdom

The advantages of obedience

Supernatural financial manifestations

If you do what He said for you to do, His supply is unstoppable. God blesses those that obey Him. *If ye be willing and obedient, ye shall eat the good of the land:*

Speedy divine intervention

If you follow God's way, you shall never be stranded in life. If you always do what is right, divine protection is guaranteed over your life and properties.

Guaranteed deliverance and protection

As a real child of God you shall have rest. God gives peace of mind to those whose mind are on Him. *"Thou wilt keep him in perfect peace, whose mind is stayed on thee: because he trusteth in thee."* **Isaiah26:3**

The Outcome of Divine Wisdom

Unstoppable progress in all areas of life

Let me conclude with this word from the Holy Spirit. The word of God you hear and believe is impotent until you put it into action. You are not a candidate of a turnaround in life until you accept responsibility and yield to obedience.

THE OUTCOME OF DIVINE WISDOM

"Happy is the man that findeth wisdom, and the man that getteth understanding. For the merchandise of it is better than the merchandise of silver, and the gain thereof than fine gold. She is more precious than rubies: and all the things thou canst desire are not to be compared unto her."

"Length of days is in her right hand; and in her left hand riches and honour. Her ways are ways of pleasantness, and all her paths are peace. She is a tree of life to them that

CHAPTER 2 : Sources of Divine Wisdom

lay hold upon her: and happy is every one that retaineth her." **Proverb3:13-18**

Anyone walking in obedience is bound to be mightily blessed. *"A faithful man shall abound with blessings."* **Proverb28:20**

THE BENEFITS OF OBEDIENCE

---------------*Long life*--------------

If you obey the word of God genuinely, you will live long, no matter the projection and assault of the enemy. (See Psalm91:16). Often we proclaim *no weapon fashioned against us shall ever prosper*. To me that's just a proposition. We must activate such strong covenant promise by doing the right thing in life.

-----*Deliverance from all evil*-----

By *the shedding blood of Jesus Christ*, you are *delivered* already. Hear this….

The Outcome of Divine Wisdom

"Who hath delivered us from the power of darkness, and hath translated us into the kingdom of his dear Son." **Col 1:13**

But to stay free from the wiles and scheme of the devil you must you must obey the commandment of God. (See Eccl8:5, 1Peter3:13)

-----*Riches and Honor*-----

We were told *"Riches and honour are with me; yea, durable riches and righteousness."* It is *Divine wisdom* to follow the principles of Jesus. As long as you obey what God is asking you to do in His word, you shall *enjoy riches and honor.*

-----*Everlasting protection*-----

Hear me out.....!!

The scripture cannot be broken. If you obey God, He will give His angels charge of

CHAPTER 2 : Sources of Divine Wisdom

your household to keep you safe in all your ways.(See Psalms91:11)

-----*Divine Ideals*-----

Divine idea brought Jacob out of Poverty. Divine Idea preserved the land of Egypt-through God's revelation to Joseph. *"And God sent me before you to preserve you a posterity in the earth, and to save your lives by a great deliverance."* **Genesis45:7**

CONCLUSION

"Wisdom hath builded her house, she hath hewn out her seven pillars."

Proverb 9:1

As you conclude reading this book. *Pray and ask God to give you divine wisdom.* The

The Outcome of Divine Wisdom

wisdom of God will give you joy, peace, and love in Jesus Mighty Name.

You have some measure of *Divine wisdom*. But from today, do not ignorantly accept and do things at impulse. Study pray and ask God for wisdom. *"Wisdom is the principal thing; therefore get wisdom: and with all thy getting get understanding."* **Proverb4:7**

"I wisdom dwell with prudence, and find out knowledge of witty inventions." **Proverb 8:12**

"Therefore if any man be in Christ, he is a new creature: old things are passed away; behold, all things are become new". 2cor5:17

Now repeat this Prayer after me

Say Father give me the grace to walk in your divine wisdom the remaining days of

CHAPTER 2 : Sources of Divine Wisdom

my life. I thank you and Praise you. In Jesus Name. **Amen**

WISDOM KEYS

Every Productive Society is a society heading to the top

Millions of Nigerians run away from Nigeria, very few Nigerians stay in Nigeria.

My decision to return Nigeria is the will of God for my life

My short coming in America after 18 years, trained me to be wise, to think, reflect and reason appropriately.

If you train your mind to reason it will train your hands to earn money.

It is absurd to use the money of the heathen to build the kingdom of the living God.

The Outcome of Divine Wisdom

Every Ministry reveals its agenda and goal either at the beginning or at the end. Be careful of your life it is your first Ministry.

The average American mind is conditioned for a continual quest to get new things and (discard the former) and throw away old things.

When I considered well, my BMW jeep became my initial deposit for the work of the ministry in Nigeria.

Everyone is waiting for you to change your mind until you change your thinking nothing changes around you.

Multiple academic degrees in other discipline gave me the chance to think, reflect, and reason

What so everyone are thinking and reflecting at the moment reveals you to the time and the now factor

CHAPTER 2 : Sources of Divine Wisdom

All events and intents are the product of precise thought processes, accurate reason every event is designed for a designated timeline

Wisdom is your ability to think, to create and invent. If you can think wise enough you will come out of penury

The distance between you and success is your creative ability to think reason and reflect accurate.

Success is the result of hard work, commitment resolve, and determination learning from past mistakes and failing.

If you organize your mind you have organized your life and destiny.

There is a thin line between success and failure. If you look above and beyond you are on your way to success.

The Outcome of Divine Wisdom

Wealth is your ability to think, power is your ability to reason and success is your ability to be informed.

If you can make use of your mind by thinking and reasoning God will make use of your life and destiny.

Think and Be Great

Reflect, Reason, think and be great

Famous people are born of woman

That you will make it is your intention; that you will survive is your resolve, that you will succeed with changes is your determination, personal efforts and hard work.

No man was born a failure. Lack of vision is the end product of failure.

Working with mental patients encourages and aspire me to be a productive observant and dedicated to my assignment.

CHAPTER 2 : Sources of Divine Wisdom

Successful people are not magicians, it is the will power combined with hard work, and determination and a resolve to succeed that make them succeed.

In the unequivocal state of the mind, intention is not a location or a position it is the state of the mind.

So many people think that they think. The mind is used to think reflect and reason. You will remain blind with your eye open until you can see with your mind by thinking.

There is no favoritism in accurate and precise calculation

Although knowledge is power, information is the key and gateway to a great future.

It will take the hand of God to move the hand of man.

The Outcome of Divine Wisdom

With the backing of the great wise God, nothing will disconnect you from your inheritance.

As long as you have wisdom and understanding of God, Satan and evil cannot manipulate your life and destiny.

You have come this far by yourself judgment and decision you have made in the past, now lean and listen to God for another dimension of greatness.

Great people are common people it is extra ordinary effort and the price of sacrifice that produces greatness.

As a mental direct care worker I saw a great pastor and a motivational speaker within myself.

Menial job does not reduce your self-worth, until you resolve to achieve greatness see greatness in all you do; you will never count in your community.

CHAPTER 2 : Sources of Divine Wisdom

The principle of Jesus will solve your gambling and addiction problems

The man of Jesus will lead you into heaven,

Everyone have their self-appraisal and what they think about you. Until you discover yourself other opinion about you will alter the real you.

Supervisors and directors are just a position in the chain of command in a work place. Never allow your supervisor hierarchy to alter your opinion about yourself.

Everyone can come out of debt if they make up their mind.

That I am not a decision maker at work does not diminish my contribution to my world.

Although it appears like it was a poor decision to accept a direct care employment at a psychiatric hospital as I reflect of my nine years of experience, it became apparent that I have learnt and experienced enough for my next assignment.

Self-encouragement and determination is a resolve of the heart.

If you are determined to make a difference, and do the things that make a difference you will eventually make a difference.

Good things do not come easy

Short cuts will cut your life short.

Those who look ahead move ahead.

Life is all about making an impact. In your life time strive to make an impact in your community.

Make friends and connect with people who are moving ahead of you in life.

CHAPTER 2 : Sources of Divine Wisdom

If you can look around well you have come a long way in your life, made a lot of difference and realized a lot of success in life.

If you are my old friend, hurry up to reach out to me before I become a stranger to you.

Everything I am blessed with inspirations from God, that change my definition and interpretation of the world around me.

I thought I was stagnant and lonely until I looked around and noticed my children running around and my wife cooking.

At 40 I resigned my Job to seek the Lord forever.

My ministry took a drastic rise to the top when the wisdom of God visited me with knowledge and understanding.

The Outcome of Divine Wisdom

You will be a better person if you understand the characteristics of your personality – your mood swings attitudes and habits.

It is the seed of love you sow into the heart of a child and a woman that you reap in due time.

Love is not selfish, love share everything including the concealed secrets of the mind.

As long as you have a prayer life and a bible; you will never feel lonely, rejected, and idle in the race of life.

When good friends disconnect from you, let them go, they might have seen something new in a different direction.

Confidence in yourself and in God is the only way to bring you out of captivity

Never train a child to waste his/her time.

The mind is the greatest assets of a great future.

CHAPTER 2 : Sources of Divine Wisdom

You walk by common sense run by principles and fly by instruction.

Those who fly in flight of life fly alone.

I have seen a tolling vehicle I have seen a tolling ship I have never seen a tolling airplane.

I exercise my judgment and make a decision every minute of the day.

Decisions are crucial, critical, and vital with reference to your future.

So many people wish for a great future. You can only work towards a great future.

Your celebrity status began when you discovered your talent. What are you good at? Work at it with all commitment.

Prayers will sustain you but the wisdom of God will prosper you.

When I met Oyedepo, his teachings changed my perspective, but when I met Ibiyeomie; His teaching changed my perception.

I will be successful in ministry if only I concentrate and focus my energy in the work of the ministry.

It took the late Dr. Vincent Pearle Norman's book to open my mind towards kingdom success.

CHAPTER 3
PRAYER OF SALVATION

"Neither is there salvation in any other: for there is none other name under heaven given among men, whereby we must be saved." Acts 4:12.

The purpose of this small book will be defeated if you finish *reading without hearing a message about your salvation.* Hear me out! Your sanctification, and Salvation is very important to God, and to your soul.

Are you saved?

To be saved we must be born again!

The word says as many as received him, to them gave He power to become the sons of God. Even to them that believe on his name.

The Outcome of Divine Wisdom

To qualify for divine visitation do the following sincerely

1) Acknowledge that you are a sinner and that He died for you.Rom3:23.

2) Repent of your sins. Acts 3:19, Luke13:5, 2Peter3:9

3) Believe in your heart that Jesus died for your sin.Romans10:10

4) Confess Jesus as the Lord over your life. Romans10:10, Acts2:21

Now repeat this Prayer after me

Say Lord Jesus, I accept you today, as my Lord and my savior, forgive me of my sins wash me with your blood. Right now, I believe, I am sanctified, I am save, I am free, I am free from the Power of sin to serve the Lord Jesus. Thank you Lord for saving me. Amen. Congratulation: YOU ARE NOW A BORN AGAIN CHRISTAIN

CHAPTER 3 : Prayer of Salvation

AGAIN I SAY TO YOU CONGRATULATION

I adjure you to watch the Spirit of God bear witness with your Spirit confirming His word with signs following. The word says The Spirit itself beareth witness with our spirit, that we are the children of God.

MIRACLE CARE OUTREACH

"…But that the members should have the same care one for another" 1cor12:25

We are all members of the body of Christ. Jesus commanded us to love our neighbor as ourselves. This includes caring for one another as a member of one body. True love is expressed in caring and giving. The word says for God so Love He gave….

Reach out to someone in need of Jesus, help someone in crisis find Christ. Look out and prove your love to Jesus by caring and inviting your friends and associates to find Jesus the Healer.

Invite your friends to our Home Care Cell Fellowship (Miracle chapel Intl Satellite fellowship) In the USA at 33 Schley Street Newark New Jersey 07112.

If you are in Nigeria—**MIRACLE OF GOD MINISTRIES**

A.K.A "**MIRACLE CHAPEL INTL**" Mpama –Egbu-Owerri Imo state Nigeria.

(Home Care Cell fellowship Group). We meet every Tuesday at 6:00pm-7:00pm.

Introduction

LIFE IS NOT ALL ABOUT DURATION BUT ITS ALL ABOUT DONATION

What does the above statement mean?....

Life consists not in accumulation of material wealth.Luke12:15. But it's all about liberality….meaning- what you can give and share with others. Proverb11:25. *When you live for others--You live forever- because you out live your generation by the legacy you live behind after you depart into glory to be with the Lord. But when you live to yourself - you are reduced to self—you are easily forgotten when you die and depart in glory. Permit me to admonish you today to live your life to be a blessing to a soul connected to you today.*

I want you to know that so many souls are connected and looking up to you, and

The Outcome of Divine Wisdom

through you so many souls will be saved and rescued from destruction. Will you disciple someone today to find Jesus Christ?

As a genuine Christian; it is your duty to evangelize Jesus Christ to all you meet on your way. Jesus is still in the healing business-Jesus is still doing miracles from time of old to now. Therefore tell someone about Jesus Christ today, disciple and bring them to Church. John 1:45 Philip findeth Nathanael….

Please to prove the sincerity of your love for God today; please become a soul winner. The dignity of your Christianity is hidden in your boldness to proclaim and evangelize Jesus Christ to all you meet on your way. There is a question mark on the integrity of your Christianity until you become a life soul winner. Invite someone to join us worship the Lord Jesus this coming Sunday. Amen

Introduction

MIRACLE OF GOD MINISTRIES

PILLARS OF THE COMMISSION

We Believe Preach and Practice the following

1) We believe and preach Salvation to every living human being

2) We believe and preach Repentance and forgiveness of sins

3) We believe and preach the baptism of the Holy Spirit and Spiritual gifts

4) We believe and teach the Prosperity

5) We believe and preach Divine Healing and Miracles (Signs & Wonder)

6) We believe and preach Faith

7) We believe and Proclaim the Power of God (Supernatural)

The Outcome of Divine Wisdom

8) We believe and Proclaim Praise & Worship to God

9) We believe and preach Wisdom

10) We believe and preach Holiness (Consecration)

11) We believe and preach Vision

12) We believe and teach the Word of God

13) We believe and teach Success

14) We believe and practice Prayer

15) We believe and teach Deliverance

This 15 stones form the Pillars of Our Commission. Become part of this church family and follow this great move of God.

MY HEART FELT PRAYER FOR YOU

As long as you are interested in Wisdom, God will give it to you. You shall succeed

CHAPTER 3 : Prayer of Salvation

in your life. I like to encourage you with a word of prayer.

It is written

"If any of you lack wisdom, let him ask of God, that giveth to all men liberally, and upbraideth not; and it shall be given him. But let him ask in faith, nothing wavering. For he that wavereth is like a wave of the sea driven with the wind and tossed."
James1:5

Now let me Pray for you:

Lord Jesus, I thank you for life and for *divine wisdom* upon my life. Father give me the grace to continue in search of *your wisdom.* I thank You for what You have done. But I praise You for what You will do for me even now. In Jesus Mighty Name.
Amen

The Outcome of Divine Wisdom

CHAPTER 4
ABOUT THE AUTHOR

Rev Franklin N Abazie is the founding and Presiding Pastor of Miracle of God Ministries with headquarters in Newark, New Jersey USA and a branch church in Owerri- Imo State Nigeria. He is following the footsteps of one of his mentors, Oral Roberts (Healing Evangelist) of the blessed memory. The Lord passed Oral Roberts healing mantle two days before he went to be with the Lord at age 91 into the hand of healing evangelist-Rev Franklin N Abazie in a vision.

In all his services the Power and Presence of God is present to heal all in his audience. He is an ordained man of God with a Healing Ministry reviving the healing

Chapter 4 : About The Author

and miracle ministry of Jesus Christ of Nazareth.

Pastor Franklin N Abazie, is called by God with a unique mandate: **"THE MOMENT IS DUE TO IMPACT YOUR WORLD THROUGH THE REVIVAL OF THE HEALING & MIRACLE MINISTRY OF JESUS CHRIST OF NAZARETH**

I AM SENDING YOU TO RESTORE HEALTH UNTO THEE AND I WILL HEAL THEE OF THY WOUNDS. SAID THE LORD OF HOST"

He is a gifted ardent Teacher of the word of God who operates also in the office of a Prophet, generating and attracting undeniable signs & wonders, special miracles and healings, with apostolic fireworks of the Holy Ghost. He is the founding and presiding senior Pastor of this fast growing Healing ministry. He has written over 86 inspirational, healing and transforming books covering almost all aspect of divine healing and life. He is happily married and blessed with children.

BOOKS BY REV FRANKLIN N ABAZIE

1) Commanding Abundance
2) The Outcome of faith
3) Understanding the secret of prevailing prayers.
4) Understanding the secret of the man God uses
5) Activating my due Season
6) Overcoming Divine Verdicts
7) The Outcome of Divine Wisdom
8) Understanding God's Restoration Mandate
9) Walking in the Victory and Authority of the truth
10) Gods Covenant Exemption
11) Destiny Restoration Pillars
12) Provoking Acceptable Praise

The Outcome of Divine Wisdom

13) Understanding Divine Judgment
14) Activating Angelic Re-enforcement
15) Provoking Un-Merited Favor
16) The Benefits of the Speaking faith
17) Understanding Divine Arrangement
18) Understanding Divine Healing
19) The Mystery of Endurance
20) Obeying Divine Instructions
21) Understanding the Voice of God
22) Never give up on Hope
23) The prevailing Power of faith
24) Understanding Divine Prosperity
25) The Reward of Prayer
26) Covenant Keys to Answered Prayers
27) Activating the Forces of Vengeance
28) Put your faith to work
29) Where is your trust?

Books By Rev Franklin N Abazie

30) The Audacity of the Blood of Jesus
31) Redeeming Your Days
32) The Force of Vision
33) Breaking the shackles of Family curses
34) Wisdom for Marriage Stability
35) Overcoming prevailing challenges
36) The Prayer solution
39) The power of Prayer
40) The effective strategy of Prayer
41) The prayer that works
42) Walking in Forgiveness
43) The prevailing power of the blood of Jesus
44) The benefit of the speaking faith.
45) Fearless faith
46) Redeeming Your Days.
47) The Supernatural Power of Prophecy

48) The Companionship of the Holy Spirit
49) Understanding Divine Judgement
50) Understanding Divine Prosperity
51) Dominating Controlling Forces
52) The winner's Faith
53) Destiny Restoration Pillars
54) Developing Spiritual Muscles
55) Inexplicable faith
56) The lifestyle of Prayer
57) Developing a positive attitude in life.
58) The mystery of Divine supply
59) Encounter with the Power of God
60) Walking in love
61) Praying in the Spirit
62) How to provoke your testimony
63) Walking in the reality of the anointing
64) The reality of new birth

65) The price of freedom
66) The Supernatural power of faith
67) The Power of Persistence
68) The intellectual components of Redemption.
69) Overcoming Fear
70) Overcoming Prevailing Challenges
71) The Power of the Grace of God.
72) My life & Ministry
73) The Mystery of Praise
74) Commanding faith
75) The Power of Bold Declaration
76) The power of Divine Intervention
77) Christian Character builder

MIRACLE OF GOD MINISTRIES

NIGERIA CRUSADE
2012

MIRACLE OF GOD MINISTRIES

NIGERIA CRUSADE
2012

MIRACLE OF GOD MINISTRIES

NIGERIA CRUSADE
2012

Wisdom Center
Forth-Worth Te
Pastors Confere
2017

www.ingramcontent.com/pod-product-compliance
Lightning Source LLC
Chambersburg PA
CBHW021130300426
44113CB00006B/364